BIG FUN

2

Mario Herrera **Barbara Hojel**

Big Fun 2

Staff credits: Staff credits: The people who made up the Big Fun team, representing editorial, production, design, manufacturing, and marketing, are Isabel Arnaud, Rhea Banker, Danielle Belfiore, Carol Brown, Kim Casey, Tracey Munz Cataldo, Dave Dickey, Gina DiLill, Christine Edmonds, Erin Ferris, Nancy Flaggman, Yoko Mia Hirano, Penny Laporte, Christopher Leonowicz, Emily Lippincott, Maria Pia Marrella, Jennifer McAliney, Kate McLoughlin, Linda Moser, Kyoko Oinuma, Leslie Patterson, Sherri Pemberton, Salvador Pereira, Pamela Pia, Juan Carlos Portillo, Jennifer Raspiller, Aristeo Redondo, Nicole Santos, Susan Saslow, Kimberley Silver, Jane Townsend, Kenneth Volcjak, Lauren Weidenman, and Carmen Zavala.

Text composition: Isabel Arnaud

Illustration credits: Blanca Nayelli Barrera, Luis Briseño, Laura Estela González, Félix León, Hugo Miranda, Javier Montiel, A Corazón Abierto

Photo credits: p. 1 (boy) Boris Bulychev/Fotolia, (papers) Irina Nartova/Shutterstock, (scissors) Vladvm/Shutterstock, (ball) Steshkin Yevgeniy/Shutterstock, (ball) Africa Studio/Fotolia, (girl) tompet80; p. 2 (top) Pamela Uyttendaele/Shutterstock, (top) Nata-Lia/Shutterste (middle) Sayid/Shutterstock, (bottom) Quang Ho/Shutterstock; p. 3 (top) Alaettin YILDIRIM/Shutterstock, (middle) marcioalves/Shutterstock, (middle) design56/Shutterstock, (bottom) Alexander Morozov/Fotolia; p. 4 (top) Alaettin YILDIRIM/Shutterstock; p. 5 (left) Vladvr Shutterstock, (center) Vereshchagin Dmitry/Shutterstock, (right) Tooykrub/Shutterstock; p. 6 (top) mma23/Shutterstock, (middle) James Thew/Fotolia, (bottom) ellenamani/Fotolia; p. 10 (left) Alexander Mak/Shutterstock, (center, Bkgd) PointaDesign/Shutterstock, (right) Mircea BEZERGHEANU/Shutterstock; p. 12 (top) 3drenderings/Shutterstock; p. 13 © Ilike/Fotolia; p. 14 (top) gosphotodesign/Shutterstock, (top) kzww/Shutterstock, (middle) Elena Stepanova/Shutterstock, (middle) Nuiiko/Shutterstock, (bottom) BananaStock/Thinksto p. 15 (top) gosphotodesign/Shutterstock, (top) Rafael Fernandez Torres/Shutterstock, (middle) Elena Stepanova/Shutterstock, (middle) Martin Valigursky/Shutterstock, (bottom) Arvind Balaraman/Shutterstock; p. 17 (left) Danny Smythe/Shutterstock, (middle) Zoonar/ Thinkstock; p. 18 (top) Excellent backgrounds/Shutterstock, center: (left) Sergey Peterman/Shutterstock, (right) 3445128471/Shutterstock, bottom: (left) martan/Shutterstock, (center) Ron and Joe/Shutterstock, (right) Eric Isselée/Thinkstock; p. 22 (top) Art_man/ Shutterstock, (middle) jps /Shutterstock, (bottom) Eric Isselee /Shutterstock, (right) gosphotodesign/Fotolia; p. 23 (left) © mitgirl/Fotolia, (right) © aragami/Fotolia; p. 25 (center) ia_64/Fotolia; p. 26 (top) Photodisc/Thinkstock, (middle) juan carlos tinjaca/Shutterstock (middle) Andresr/Shutterstock, (bottom) Photodisc/Thinkstock; p. 27 (top) Denys Prokofyev/Thinkstock, (middle) V. J. Matthew/Shutterstock, (middle) Nikonboy/Shutterstock, (bottom) Eric Isselée/Thinkstock, (bottom) cynoclub/Fotolia; p. 30 top (left) Helder Almeida/ Thinkstock, (right) Petrenko Andriy/Shutterstock, center: (left) Elena Schweitzer/Fotolia, (right) Africa Studio/Shutterstock, bottom: (left) bloomua/Shutterstock, (middle) Markus Mainka/Fotolia, (middle) Eric Isselee/Shutterstock, (right) CLIPAREA l Custom media/ Shutterstock; p. 34 (top) Serjio74/Shutterstock, (middle) Keneva Photography/Shutterstock, (bottom) Calin Tatu/Shutterstock, (left) © Francis González/Fotolia; p. 35 (center) Samuel Borges Photography/Shutterstock; p. 37 (left) Ilike/Shutterstock, (top) Ivonne Wierink/ Shutterstock, (middle) Timof/Shutterstock, (middle) © Ingram Publishing/Thinkstock, (bottom) Jupiterimages/Thinkstock; p. 38 (top) ilker canikligil/Shutterstock, (middle) © Ingram Publishing/Thinkstock, (middle) Jupiterimages/Thinkstock, (bottom) Julian Rovagnati/ Shutterstock; p. 39 (top) DM7/Shutterstock, (middle) Timof/Shutterstock, (middle) Ivonne Wierink/Shutterstock, (bottom) djedzura/Shutterstock; p. 41 (left) bogdan ionescu/Shutterstock, (middle) Iwona Grodzka /Shutterstock, (right) Stepan Bormotov/Shutterstock; p. 42 (top) Eric Isselee/Shutterstock, (middle) Jenny Sturm/Shutterstock, (middle) Marina Jay/Shutterstock, (bottom) gillmar/Shutterstock; p. 46 (left) Stockbyte/Thinkstock, (center) Comstock/Thinkstock, (right) Comstock/Thinkstock, (left) Stephanie Frey/Shutterstock; p. 47 (EW CHEE GUAN/Shutterstock, (right) Jose Manuel Gelpi/Fotolia; p. 49 (girl) Liudmila P. Sundikova/Shutterstock, (boy) Ilike/Shutterstock, (corn) Sergii Figurnyi/Shutterstock, (apple) Nattika/Shutterstock, (salad) siamionau pavel/Shutterstock, (fish) Africa Studio/Shutters p. 50 (top) Dan Peretz/Shutterstock, (middle) Africa Studio/Shutterstock, (middle) Valentina Razumova/Shutterstock, (bottom) siamionau pavel/Shutterstock; p. 51 (top) Sergii Figurnyi/Shutterstock, (middle) Max Krasnov/Shutterstock, (middle) homydesign/Shutterstock, (bottom) tore2527/Shutterstock; p. 53 (left) Yeko Photo Studio/Shutterstock, (center) victoriaKh/Shutterstock, (right) Thomas Hecker/Shutterstock; p. 54 (top) saddako/Shutterstock, (left) Sergey Peterman/Shutterstock, (right) Olga Popova/Shutterstock; p. 55 (left) Pears Education, (center) Nattika/Shutterstock, (top right) topseller/Shutterstock, (center right) Gemenacom/Shutterstock; p. 56 (left) Valentina Razumova/Shutterstock, (right) Max Krasnov/Shutterstock; p. 58 fruits: (top) Max Krasnov/Shutterstock, (middle) Valentina Razumo Shutterstock, (bottom) Gemenacom/Shutterstock, seeds: (top) mates/Fotolia, (bottom) LU HUANFENG/Shutterstock; p. 59 (center) Susanna Price/DKimages; p. 61 (girl) aishka/Shutterstock, (boy) Varina and Jay Patel/Shutterstock, (raincoat) Zoonar/Thinkstock, (boots) sunsetman/Shutterstock, (hat) Marek R. Swadzba/Shutterstock, (swimsuit) Ruslan Kudrin/Shutterstock; p. 62 (top) Ruslan Kudrin/Shutterstock, (middle) sagir/Shutterstock, (middle) Shapiro Svetlana/Shutterstock, (bottom) Marek R. Swadzba/Shutterstock; p. 63 (top) O Zaskochenko/Shutterstock, (middle) Zoonar/Thinkstock, (middle) BradCalkins/Thinkstock, (bottom) Andrei Radzkou/Thinkstock; p. 65 (top) Richard Peterson/Shutterstock, (bottom) Africa Studio/Shutterstock; p. 66 (top) Korionov/Shutterstock, (left) Valua Vitaly/ Shutterstock, (right) rnl/Shuttersock; p. 70 (top) © doris oberfrank/Fotolia, (left) Michael J Thompson/Shutterstock, (middle) Dr Ajay Kumar Singh/Shutterstock, (right) louisjoseph/Fotolia; p. 71 (center) TuTheLens/Shutterstock; p. 73 (girl) Andrey Lipko/Shutterstock, (hon Eric Isselée/Fotolia, (lamb) Eric Isselee/Shutterstock, (barn) Andrea Danti/Shutterstock, (rabbit) Eric Isselee/Shutterstock, (hen) sval7/Shutterstock; p. 74 (top) Eric Isselee/Shutterstock, (middle) Stefan Petru Andronache/Shutterstock, (middle) sval7/Shutterstock, (bottom Eric Isselee/Shutterstock; p. 75 (top) Bjorn Heller/Shutterstock, (middle) KennStilger47/Shutterstock, (middle) Erik Lam/Shutterstock, (bottom) Eric Isselee/Shutterstock; p. 77 (top) Bjorn Heller/Shutterstock, (bottom) Andrea Danti/Shutterstock; p. 78 (top) oxilixo/Fotolia, (left) Erik Lam/Shutterstock, (right) © Yuri Arcurs/Fotolia; p. 82 (center) Africa Studio/Shutterstock; p. 83 (left) In Green/Shutterstock, (right) DenisNata/Shutterstock; p. 85 (left) Glenda/Shutterstock, (right) wacpan/Shutterstock; p. 90 (top) bluehand/Shutterstock, (left) Vladimir Jotov/Shutterstock, (right) Alan Poulson Photography/Shutterstock; p. 94 (left) deviantART/Fotolia, (right) Yuriy Mazur/Fotolia; p. 95 Shane Trotter/Shutterstock; p. 97 Digital Vision/Thinkstock; p. 98 Dmitry Naumov/Shutterstock; p. 99 MidoSemsem/Shutterstoc p. 109 (top) James Thew/Fotolia, (left) ellenamani/Fotolia, (right) mma23/Fotolia; p. 111 (top) Caleb Foster/Shutterstock, (middle) StockLite/Shutterstock, (bottom) Cindy Jenkins/Shutterstock; p. 113 (top) Tom Suarez/Fotolia, (middle) Birdiegal/Shutterstock, (bottom) Mik Truchon/Shutterstock; p. 115 (seal) Nicram Sabod/Shutterstock, (duck) Africa Studio/Shutterstock, (monkey) Marina Jay/Shutterstock, (kitten) Jiri Hera/Shutterstock, (eyes) Stephanie Frey/Shutterstock, (ears) Voronin76/Shutterstock, (hands) Nuiiko/Shutterstock; p. 117 (top) siamionau pavel/Shutterstock, (middle) Christian Musat/Shutterstock, (bottom) mizio70/Shutterstock, p. 119 (top left) Paul Matthew Photography/Shutterstock, (middle left) Excellent backgrounds/Shutterstock, (center top) Markus Mainka/Shutterstock, (middle Kalmatsuy/Shutterstock, (center bottom) Top Photo Group/Thinkstock, (top right) Anke van Wyk/Shutterstock, (middle right) MustafaNC/Shutterstock, (bottom right) Kavee Vivii/Shutterstock; p. 121 (top left) Bjorn Heller/Shutterstock, (middle left) Sherry Yates Young LP Shutterstock, (center top) oznuroz/Shutterstock, (center) eans/Shutterstock, (center bottom) Eric Isselée/Thinkstock, (top right) Peredniankina/Fotolia, (middle right) saied shahin kiya/Shutterstock, (bottom right) saied shahin kiya/Shutterstock; p. 123 (center) Denise Kap Fotolia, (center bottom) Ljupco Smokovski/Shutterstock, (right) deviantART/Fotolia.

Stickers: p. 1 Unit 1: (top) Nata-Lia/Shutterstock, (middle) marcioalves/Shutterstock, (middle) Africa Studio/Fotolia, (bottom) design56/Shutterstock; Unit 2: (top) BananaStock/Thinkstock; Unit 3: (top) juan carlos tinjaca/Shutterstock, (middle) Andresr/Shutterstock, (bott DenisNata/Shutterstock; Unit 4: (top) Ivonne Wierink/Shutterstock, (bottom) Ingram Publishing/Thinkstock; Unit 5: (top) Dan Peretz/Shutterstock, (bottom) Africa Studio/Shutterstock; Unit 6: (top) © Getty Images/Thinkstock, (bottom) Lucy Liu/Shutterstock; Unit 7: (top) Bjorn Heller/Shutterstock, (middle) Erik Lam/Shutterstock, (bottom) Eric Isselee/Shutterstock.

Consultants and reviewers: Leticia Aguilar Maldonado, Mexico City • Jocelyn Arcos Morales, Mexico City • Irma Canales Garrido, Mexico City • María Alejandra Escobedo Maciel, Mexico City • Laura García López, Mexico City • Marís Gómez Palestino, Escuela Mexicana Bilingüe, Mexico City • Rosa Lirio Cepeda Pérez, Institución Asunción de México, Mexico City • Choonje Lee, PLS Korea • Angel López, Colegio Monte Rosa, Mexico City • Wendy Paola Méndez Cruz, Mexico City • Araceli Mendoza Negrete, Mexico City • Fabiola Mora Gálvez, Universidad Motolinia, Mexico City • Georgina Mora Gálvez, Universidad Motolinia, Mexico City • Rocío Morales Romero, Mexico City • Leticia Aurora Moreno González, C.D.I.I. Melanie Kleine, Mexico City • Pedro Olmos Medina, Colegio Maestr Carlos Chávez, Mexico City • R. Norma Pérez Rodríguez, Mexico City • Karen Polanco, Colegio Monte Rosa, Mexico City • Helen Santoyo Orozco, Escuela Cristóbal Colón, Mexico City • María Guadalupe Torres Patiño, Escuela Cristóbal Colón, Mexico City

Music credits: Music composed by John Farrell, Hope River Music, www.johnfarrell.net, and Jeff Miller, Grant's Corners, Walden, NY, assisted by Conway Chewning. Music and vocal recordings produced by Jeff Miller and John Farrell. Recorded and mixed by Jeff Mill at Grant's Corners, Remote Recordings, Yorktown Heights, NY, and Hillsdale, NY. Song lyrics by Barbara Hojel, with contributions by John Farrell. Children's vocal performance directed by Lorraine Cich. Child vocal performers: Julia Apostolou, Aisha Bhakta, Emma Halderman, Cassidy Kenney, Juliana Moscati; adult vocal performers: Lorraine Cich, John Farrell, Maggie Farrell, Ann Marie Lord. Additional composition and editing: Eastern Sky Media Services, Inc. Casselberry, Florida. Produced by Jon W. Reames and David E. Brov

Recording and Audio Production services: CityVox, LLC.

Printed in China
ISBN-10: 0-13-343743-4
ISBN-13: 978-0-13-343743-0

13 17

CONTENTS

Cutouts and Stickers included!

BIG FUN
Song

Chorus →

From the sky to the ground
And all the way around—
We can have big fun!
If there's rain, if there's sun,
Let's play with everyone.
We can have big, big fun!

Take a walk outside.
Our world is big and wide.
There are flowers and trees,
And yellow bumblebees.
Buzz, buzz, buzz!

(Chorus)

Join your hands with me.
Let's see what we can see!
Then take a closer look.
We'll learn beyond our book.
Look, oh, look!

(Chorus)

MY SCHOOL

1 **Look and predict. Listen.**

Find the balls!

2 Listen and say. Find and match.

scissors

markers

shelves

books

2 Vocabulary Presentation: *scissors, markers, shelves, books*
Language Presentation: *What are these? They are (scissors).* Review: *What is this? It is (a book).*

3 Listen and say. Find and match.

box

ball

hoops

jungle gym

Vocabulary Presentation: *box, ball, hoops, jungle gym; inside, outside*
Language Practice: *What are these? They are (hoops).* Review: *What is this? It is a (ball).*

4 ✂ **Cut out. Look and trace. Paste.**

 —————————  —————————

 —————————  —————————

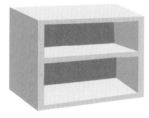 —————————  —————————

Vocabulary Practice: *box, ball, jungle gym, boy, shelves, books*; Review prepositions: *in, on*
Language Review: *This is (a box). These are (shelves).*

5 Listen and say. Trace numbers, count, and match.

1   2   3

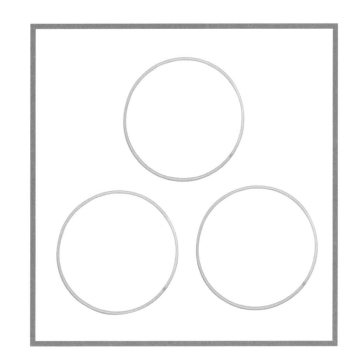

Math Connection: *Numbers 1, 2, 3*; Review: *This is/These are*

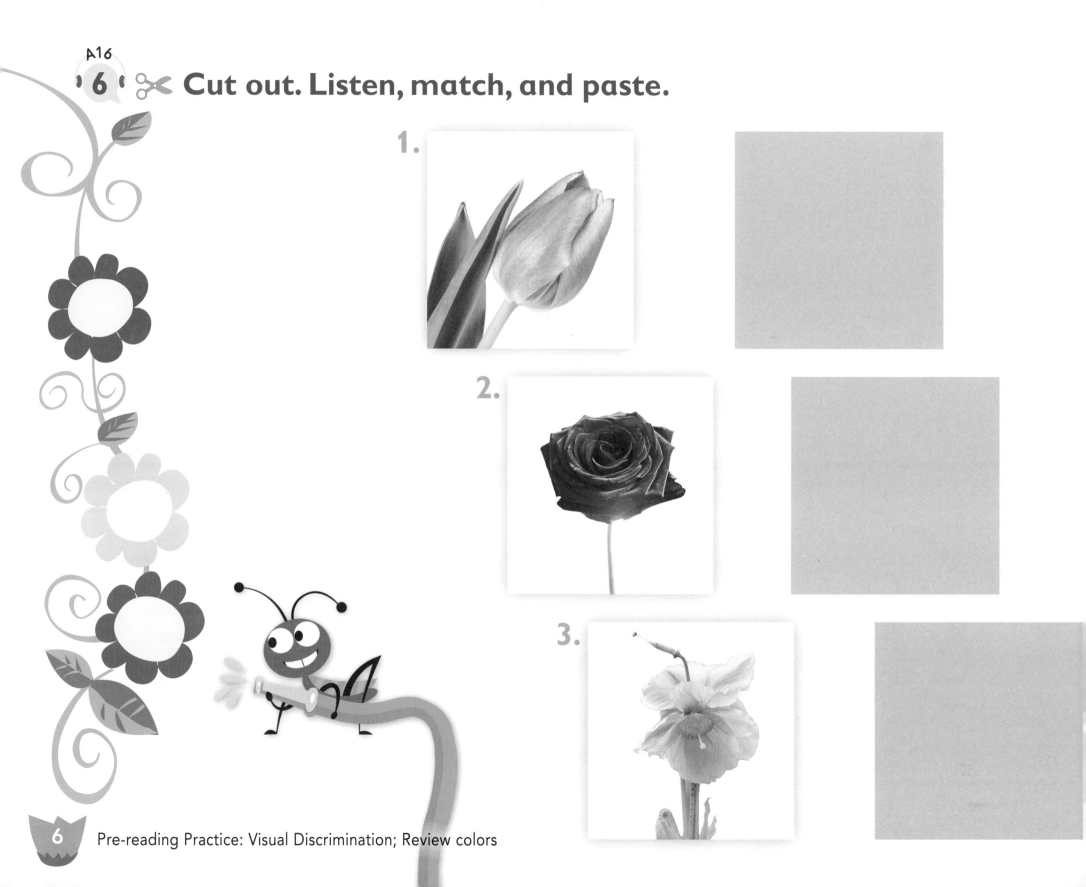

6 ✂ Cut out. Listen, match, and paste.

1.

2.

3.

Pre-reading Practice: Visual Discrimination; Review colors

4

 Your turn. Draw and color.

Draw and color.

1

 It's a ball!

 Very good!

 What are these?

 They are puppets!

2

3

VALUES

7 Trace and draw yourself.

Find a box!

Values: Respect the teacher and listen.
Vocabulary Practice: *shelves, scissors, markers, books, box*; **FIND IT:** *box*

8 Look closely. Color the frame around the snail's trail.

What are these?

Critical Thinking: Snails make trails.
Science Words: *snail, trail*

PROJECT

Make a Snail

Project: Draw a snail and make its trail.
Science and Art Connections

9 Draw your face. Stick and say.

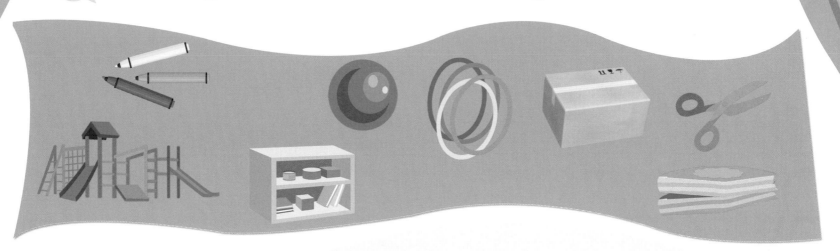

They are _____ .

GO TO
SHOW
TIME
Page 100

A5 & A21

1 **Look and predict.** Listen.

Find the bells!

2 Listen and say. Find and match.

tongue

nose

ear

hands

eyes

I smell with my nose.

Vocabulary Presentation: *tongue, nose, ear, hands, eyes*
Language Presentation: *What do you (smell) with? I (smell) with my (nose).*

3 Listen and say. Find and match.

smell

see

taste

touch

hear

Vocabulary Presentation: *smell, see, taste, touch, hear;* Vocabulary Practice: *eyes, nose, ears, hands, tongue*
Language Practice: *What do you (taste) with? I (taste) with my (tongue).*

4 ✂ **Cut out. Look and paste.**

Vocabulary Practice: *see, smell, taste, hear, touch; campfire, flower, soup, piano, blocks;* Review: colors
Language Presentation: *I see (a campfire).*

5 Listen and say. Trace numbers, count, and match.

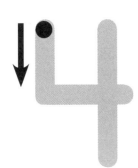  

Math Connection: *Numbers 4, 5, 6*; Review: *This is/They are*; **FIND IT**: *squares*

6 Listen and match. Say.

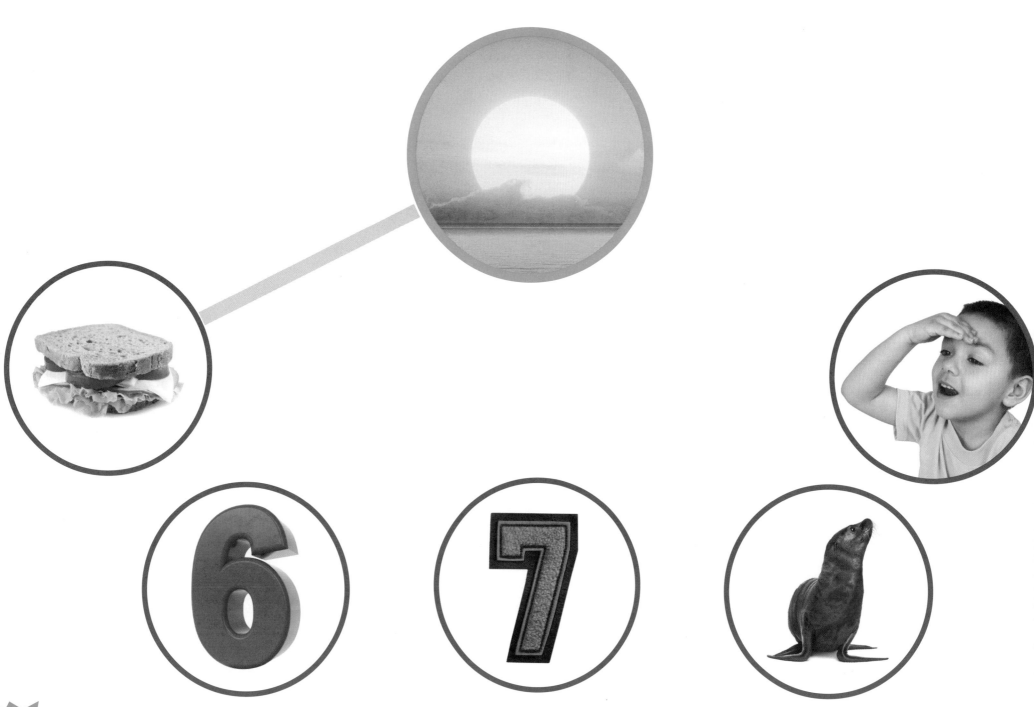

Pre-reading Practice: Initial Sound /s/; Phonics Words: *sun, sandwich, six, seven, seal, see*

4

 What is this?   Mmmm. I taste apple with my tongue!

 What is this?   I don't know. I see with my eyes.

1

2  What is this?   I don't know. I smell with my nose.

 What is this?   I don't know! I want to taste it! 3

7 Who is polite? Circle.

Values: Be polite and wait for your turn.
FIND IT: *ears*

8 ✂ **Look closely. Cut out and paste.**

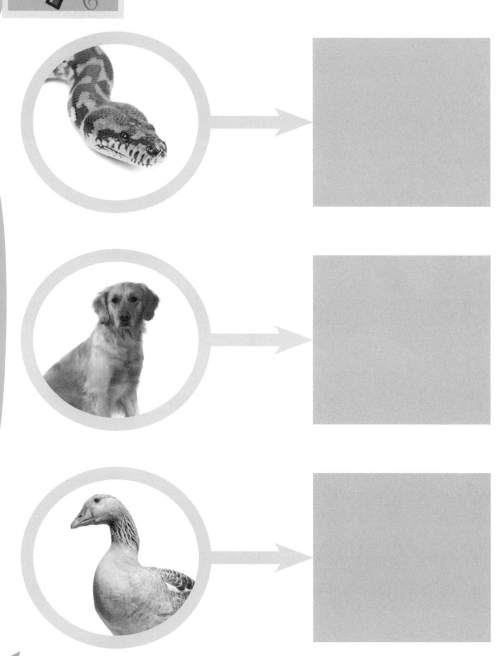

What do
you taste with?

Critical Thinking: Animals use tongues to taste.
Science Words: *tongue, taste buds*

Taste with Your Tongue!

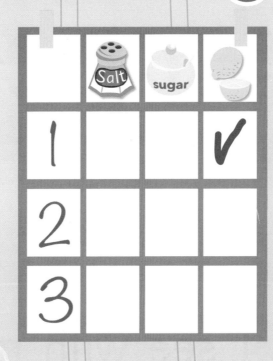

Project: Experiment with different tastes.
Science Connection

9 **Draw your face. Stick and say.**

I see with my _____ .

GO TO
SHOW
TIME
Page 101

3 MY FAMILY

1 **Look and predict. Listen.**

Find the babies!

2 Listen and say. Find and match.

grandfather

grandmother

aunt

uncle

Vocabulary Presentation: *grandfather, grandmother, aunt, uncle*; Vocabulary Review: *grandparents*
Language Review: *Who is (she)? (She) is my (grandmother). Who are they? They are my (grandparents).*

3 Listen and say. Find and match.

cousin

house

apartment

pets

Vocabulary Presentation: *cousin, house, apartment, pets (cat, dog)*
Language Review: *What is this? It is my (house). What are these? They are (my pets).*

4 ✂ **Cut out. Paste and say.**

Vocabulary Practice: *grandmother, uncle, pets (cat, fish, bird, dog), house, apartment*
Language Presentation: *Where does (Grandmother) live? In (a house).*

5 Listen and say. Trace numbers, count, and match.

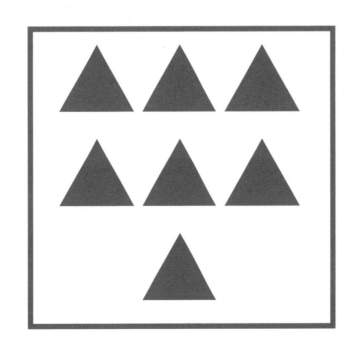

Math Connection: *Numbers 7, 8, 9*; Review: *This is/These are*; colors

6 Listen and match. Say.

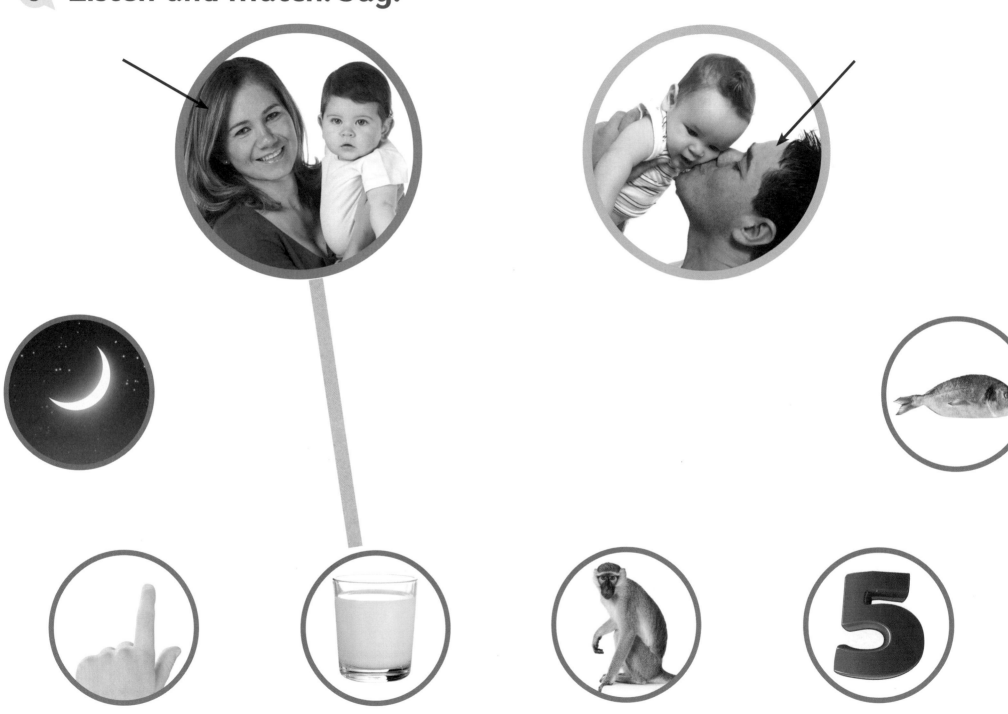

Pre-reading Practice: Initial Sounds /m/ and /f/; Phonics Words: *mother, moon, milk, monkey; father, finger, five, fish*

Show and Tell

 They are all my family!

 Is she your mother?

No, she is not! She is my aunt.

 Who is he?

He is my cousin!

 Who is he?

He is my uncle!

VALUES

7 **Draw someone in your family.**

Find the grandfather!

Values: Show you appreciate family members.
Vocabulary Practice: *grandmother, grandfather;* **FIND IT:** *grandfather*

AMAZING

8 ✂ **Look closely. Cut out and paste.**

Critical Thinking: Birds make different houses.
Science Words: *nest, swallow, eagle, hummingbird, robin*

Make a Paper Nest

What lives in a nest?

Project: Weave paper to make a nest.
Science and Art Connections

9 **Stick and say.**

She is my _____ .

 GO TO SHOW TIME Page 102

MY TOYS

1 Look and predict. Listen.

Find the slides!

2 Listen and say. Find and match.

swing

tricycle

car

slide

I have a tricycle.

Vocabulary Presentation: *swing, tricycle, car, slide*
Language Presentation: *What do you have? I have (a tricycle).*

3 Listen and say. Find and match.

action figure

blocks

game

play house

I have an action figure.

Vocabulary Presentation: *action figure, blocks, game, play house*;
Language Practice: *What do you have? I have (an action figure).*

4 Look and color.

Vocabulary Presentation: *gray*; Vocabulary Practice: *action figure, play house, slide, swing*; Review: colors
Language Presentation: *Do you have (a play house)? Yes, I do./No, I don't.*

5 Listen and say. Trace numbers, count, and match.

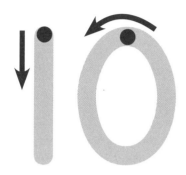

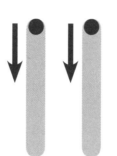

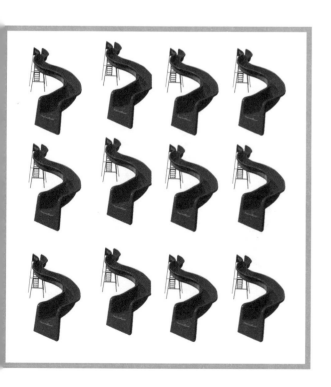

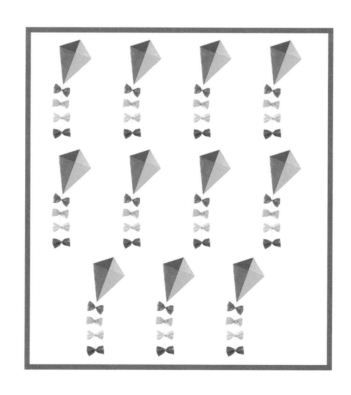

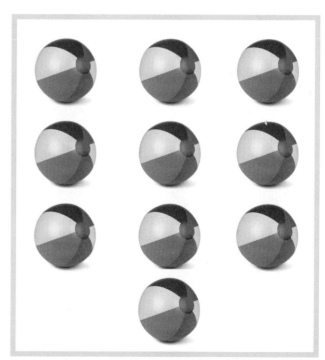

6 ✂ Cut out, listen, and paste. Sing.

1.

2.

3.

4.

Pre-reading Practice: Animal Sounds: monkey (*oo ahh*), duck (*quack*), seal (*arf*), cat (*meow*)
Big and little animals make sounds, and big and small letters stand for sounds.

A61 # Outdoor Fun

4

 Now I have a puppet-kite!

 Hello. What do you have?

 I have a puppet and blocks.

1

2

What do you have?

I have a kite.

I want the puppet, please!

3

7 Color blocks. What do you see?

Find the puppets.

Values: Share toys to make something together.
Vocabulary Practice: *play house, blocks, puppet, doll, action figure*; **FIND IT:** *puppets*

8 ✂ **Look closely. Cut out and paste.**

What is this?

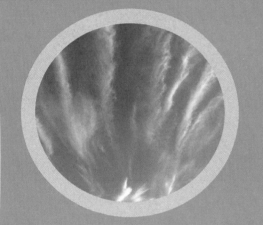

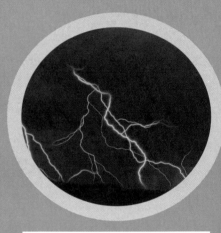

Critical Thinking: Study how the sky changes.
Science Words: *clouds, rain, lightning, thunder*

9 Draw your face. Stick and say.

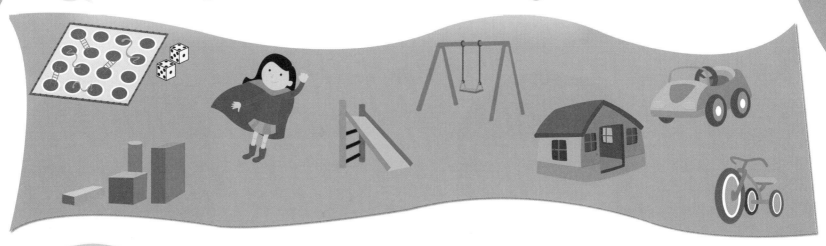

I have a _____ .

GO TO SHOW TIME Page 103

FOOD

1 Look and predict. Listen.

Find the watermelon!

2 Listen and say. Find and match.

meat

fish

oranges

salad

I like fish.

Vocabulary Presentation: *meat, fish, oranges, salad*
Language Presentation: *What do you like? I like (fish).*

3 Listen and say. Find and match.

corn

watermelon

potatoes

chicken

UNIT 5

51

Vocabulary Presentation: *corn, watermelon, potatoes, chicken*
Language Presentation: *Do you like (corn)? Yes, I do./No, I don't.* Language Practice: *What do you like? I like (fish).*

4 ✂ **Cut out, choose, and paste food. Color the drink.**

Vocabulary Practice: *meat, fish, chicken, corn, potatoes, salad, milk, lemonade, juice*
Language Presentation: *What do you want to eat? I want (chicken), please.*

5 Listen and say. Trace numbers, count, and match.

 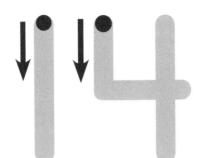 

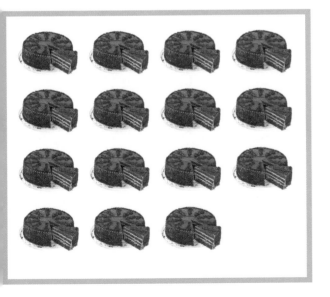 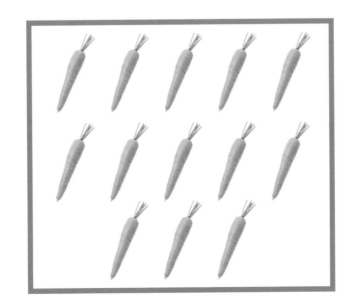 

Math Connection: *Numbers 13, 14, 15; Vocabulary Practice*

UNIT 5
53

6 ✂ **Listen and say. Cut out and paste. Trace and write.**

S s S s

Pre-reading and Pre-writing Practice: *Ss*
Phonics Words: *soup, salad, sandwich, sun, socks, seal*

I like fruit salad!

4

I Like Apples

I like apples.

I like oranges.

2

I like watermelon.

3

7 **Color the scene showing good table manners.**

Values: Use table manners.
FIND IT: *salt*

8 Look and say. Match.

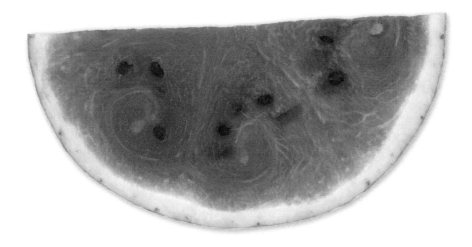

fruit

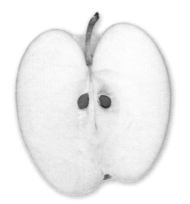

seeds

Critical Thinking: There are seeds in fruit. Plants grow from seeds.
Science Words: *fruit, seeds*

Plant a Seed

Think big!

seeds

Project: Plant a seed and watch it grow.
Science Connection

9 Draw your face. Stick and say.

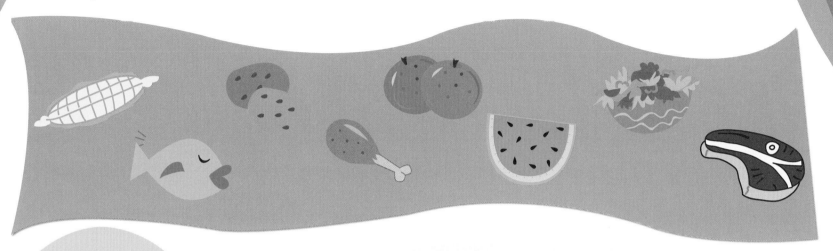

I like _____ .

GO TO
SHOW
TIME
Page 104

MY CLOTHES

1 Look and predict. Listen.

Find the umbrellas!

2 Listen and say. Find and match.

bathing suit

shorts

sandals

hat

62 Vocabulary Presentation: *bathing suit, shorts, sandals, hat*
Language Presentation: *What is (she) wearing? (She) is wearing (a bathing suit).*

jacket

raincoat

boots

umbrella

3 **Listen and say. Find and match.**

B17–18

She is wearing a bathing suit.

Vocabulary Presentation: *jacket, raincoat, boots, umbrella*
Language Practice: *What is (he) wearing? (He) is wearing (a jacket).* Language Review: *What does (he) have? (He) has (an umbrella).*

4 Look and match. Say.

Vocabulary Presentation: *sunny, rainy, windy*; Vocabulary Review: *T-shirt, sweater, pants*
Language Presentation: *It is (sunny).* Language Practice: *What is (he) wearing? (He) is wearing (shorts).*

5 ✂ Listen and say. Cut out and paste. Trace and count.

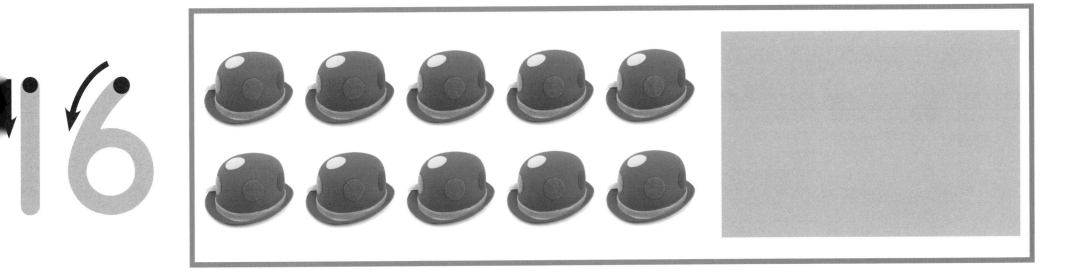

Math Connection: *Numbers 16, 17*
Review: *How many (hats) can you see? I can see (16) hats.*

6 ✂ Listen and say. Cut out and paste. Trace and write.

moon

milk

mother

mouth

muffin

meat

Mm Mm

Pre-reading and Pre-writing Practice: *Mm*
Phonics Words: *moon, milk, mother, mouth, muffin, meat*

Copyright © 2014 by Pearson Education, Inc.

How Many?

Sweaters

hats

socks

sweater

How many sweaters do you see?

I see 1 BIG sweater!

4

What do you see?

1

2

 How many hats do you see?

 I see 4 hats.

 How many socks do you see?

 I see 6 socks.

3

7 Who is helping? Look and color.

Find the hat!

Values: Help others.
Vocabulary Practice: *raincoat, hat, umbrella, boots*; **FIND IT:** *hat*

AMAZING

8 ✂ **Look closely. Cut out and paste.**

Critical Thinking: Feathers help birds.
Science Words: *seagulls, robin, parrot, peacock*

Make a Bird Puppet

Your bird can fly!

UNIT 6
71

Project: Make a bird finger puppet.
Art and Science Connections

9 Draw your face. Stick and say.

He/She is wearing

_____ .

GO TO
SHOW
TIME
Page 105

ANIMALS

1 **Look and predict. Listen.**

Find the tractors!

Unit Preview; **FIND IT** in the unit: *tractors*   73

2 Listen and say. Find and match.

cow

rabbit

chicken

sheep

74 Vocabulary Presentation: *cow, rabbit, chicken, sheep; under, next to*
Language Presentation: *Where is the (chicken)? Here it is. It is (under the tree).*

3 Listen and say. Find and match.

tractor

barn

lamb

horse

Vocabulary Presentation: *tractor, barn, lamb, horse*; Vocabulary Practice: *cat; under, next to, in*
Language Presentation: *Where are the (lambs)? Here they are.*

4 Listen. Look and trace. Say.

Vocabulary Practice: *cat, horse, girl, boy, dogs, ducks*
Language Presentation: *This is a (cat). That is a (horse). These are (dogs). Those are (ducks).*

5 ✂ **Listen and say. Cut out and paste. Trace and count.**

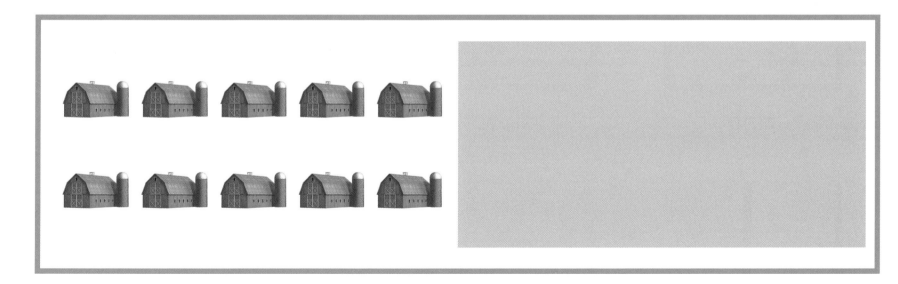

6 ✂ **Listen and say. Cut out and paste. Trace and write.**

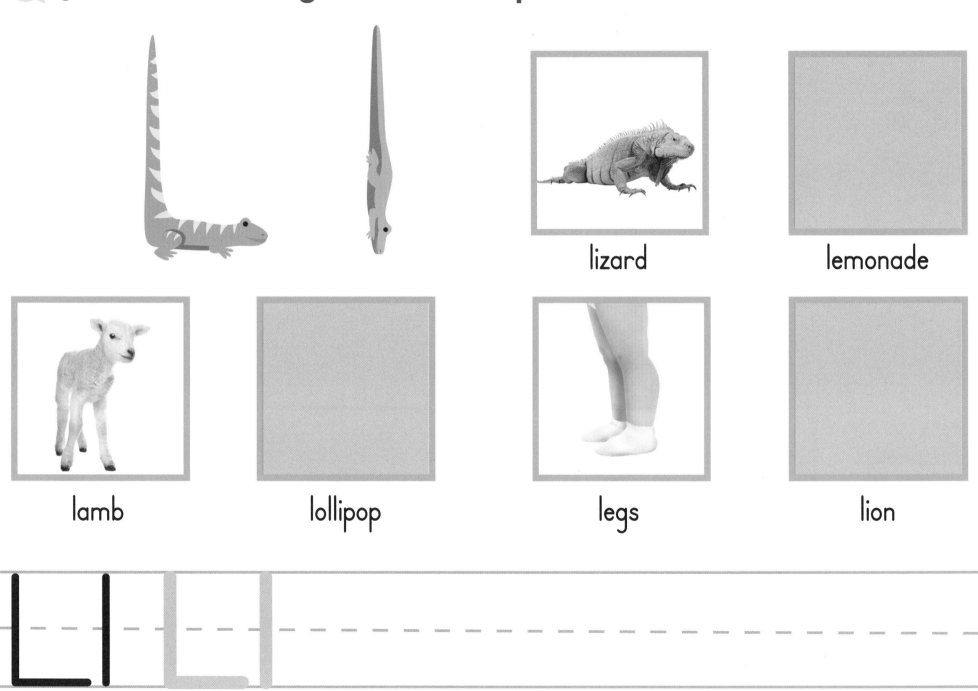

lizard

lemonade

lamb

lollipop

legs

lion

Pre-reading and Pre-writing Practice: *Ll*
Phonics Words: *lizard, lemonade, lamb, lollipop, legs, lion*

Where Are the Lambs?

4

 Here are the lambs.

 I have a lamb, too!

 Where are the rabbits?

 **Here they are.**

1

 Where are the lambs?

2

 I see a lamb in the sky. Come with me!

3

Find a cow!

7 How do you take care of an animal? Draw.

Values: We take care of animals.
FIND IT: *cow*

8 ✂ **Look closely. Cut out and paste the cutouts in order.**

1

2

3

Wow! That's amazing!

Critical Thinking: Chicks come from eggs.
Science Words: *egg, eggshell, chick*

PROJECT
Make a Chick Card

Where is the chick?

Here it is!

Project: Make a card showing a chick inside an egg.
Art and Science Connections

9 **Draw your face. Stick and say.**

Where are the _____ ?

GO TO
SHOW
TIME
Page 106

Review; Assessment for Learning

MY WORLD

A5 & B39

1 Look and predict. Listen.

2 Listen and say. Find and match.

restaurant

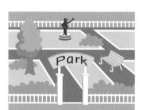

park

fire station

school

Vocabulary Presentation: *restaurant, park, fire station, school*; Vocabulary Practice: *next to*
Language Presentation: *Where is the (restaurant)? It is over there. It is (next to) the (fire station).*

3 Listen and say. Find and match.

hospital

police station

store

supermarket

Where is the school?

It is next to the hospital.

Vocabulary Presentation: *hospital, police station, store, supermarket; in front of, behind*; Vocabulary Practice: *next to*
Language Presentation: *Where is the (park)? It is (behind) the (store).*

4 Look and trace. Say.

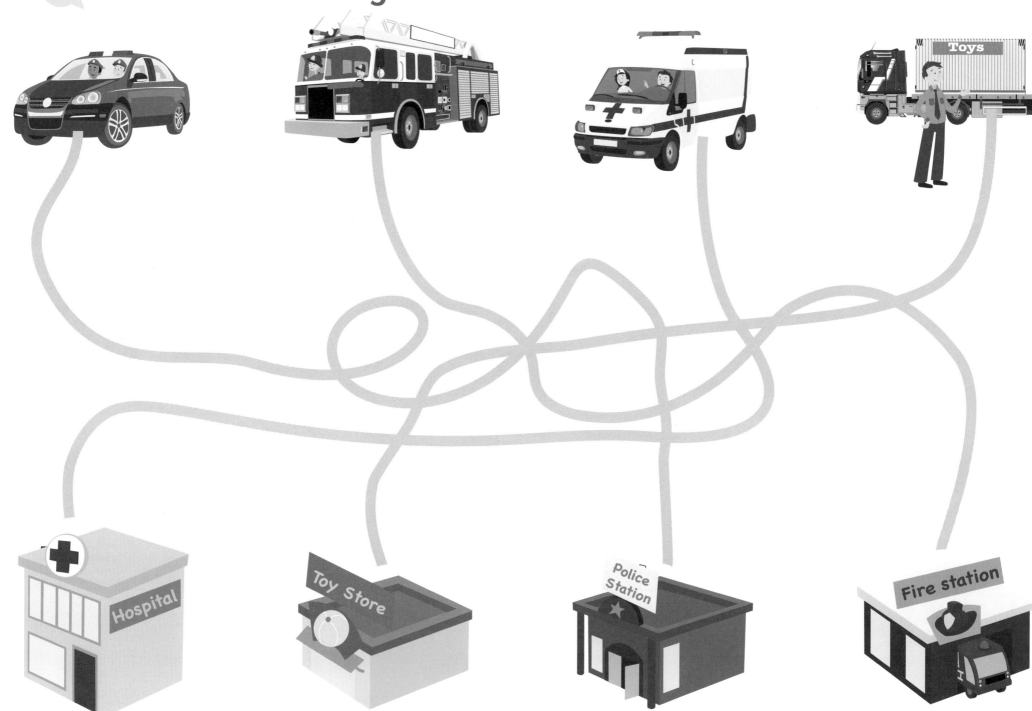

Vocabulary Presentation: *police car, fire truck, ambulance, truck, toy store*
Language Presentation: *Where is the (fire truck) going? It's going to the (fire station).*

5 ✂ **Listen and say. Cut out and count. Paste and trace.**

20  +

1 2 3 4 5 6 7 8 9 10

11 12 13 14 15 16 17 18 19 20

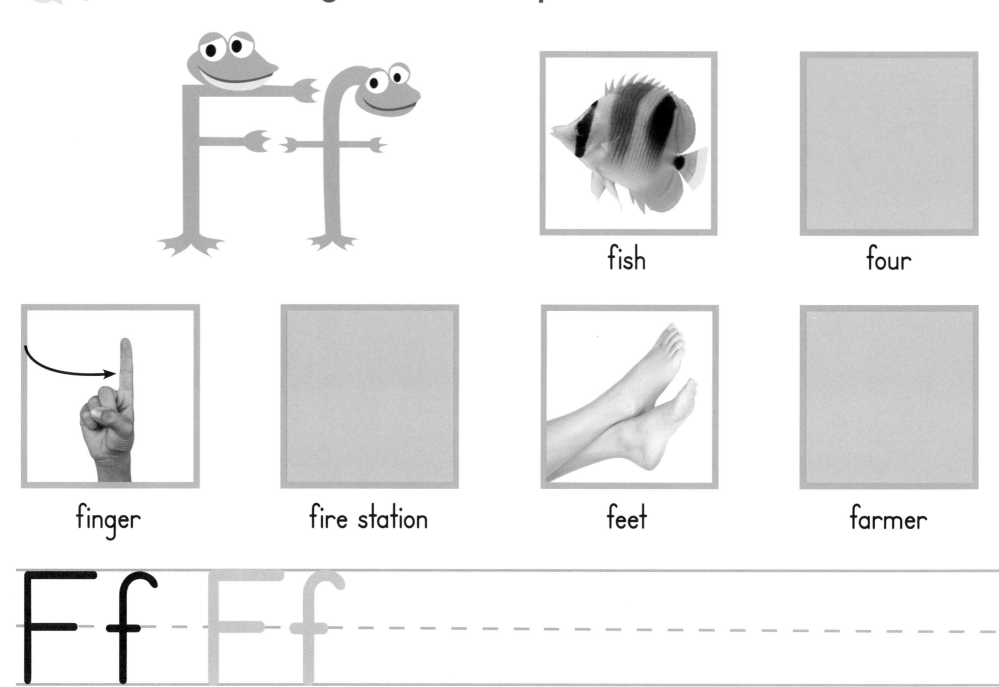

6 ✂ **Listen and say. Cut out and paste. Trace and write.**

Ff

fish

four

finger

fire station

feet

farmer

F f   F f   F f

Pre-reading and Pre-writing Practice: *Ff*
Phonics Words: *fish, four, finger, fire station, feet, farmer*

Shopping with Mommy

4

 Where is Tim?

He is sleeping in the chair!

Where are the chairs?

 They are over there.

1

 Can I sit down?

Yes, you can.

2

Where are the tables?

 They are next to the chairs.

3

I recycle.

1. 2. 3. 4. 5.

8 ✂ **Look closely. Cut out and paste.**

1

2

3

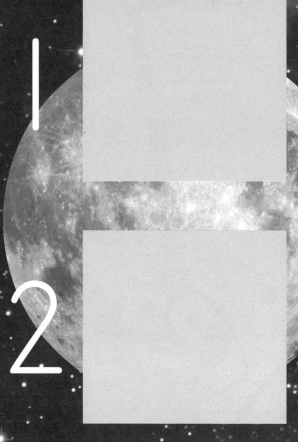

Where is the moon?

It's over there!

Critical Thinking: The moon looks different every night.
Science Words: *crescent moon, half moon, full moon*

Make a Telescope

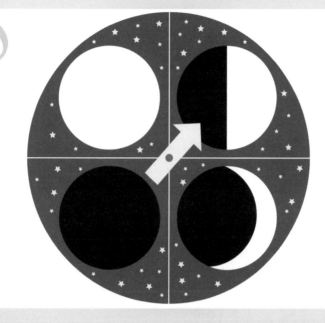

Project: Make a telescope and observe the moon.
Science and Art Connections

9 Draw your face. Stick and say.

Park

Fire Station

Police Station

Hospital

Restaurant

School

Toys

Supermarket

Where is the _____ ?

GO TO
SHOW
TIME
Page 107

SHOW TIME!

Listen and sing.

Find the flowers!

Make a Flower Mask

1.

2.

3.

Show Time Project: Make a flower mask.

PROJECT Make Scenery

1.

2.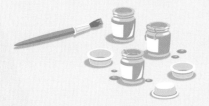

3.

Show Time Project: Make scenery.

SHOW TIME

Unit 1 MY SCHOOL

Think about the unit. Draw.

Welcome!

SHOW TIME

Unit 2 MY SENSES

Think about the unit. Draw.

Hello!

Unit 3 MY FAMILY

Think about the unit. Draw.

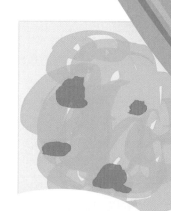

Paint a garden background.

SHOW TIME

Unit 4 MY TOYS

Think about the unit. Draw.

Have fun!

SHOW TIME

Unit 5 FOOD

Think about the unit. Draw.

Use props!

Unit 6 MY CLOTHES

Think about the unit. Draw.

Make costumes!

SHOW TIME

Unit 7 ANIMALS

Think about the unit. Draw.

Thank you!

SHOW TIME

Unit 8 MY WORLD

Think about the unit. Draw.

UNIT 9

BIG

FUN

2

Great!

has completed **Level 2!**

_____

_____

Teacher

page 4   **page 6**

 **Cutouts for Unit 2**

page 16

**page 22**

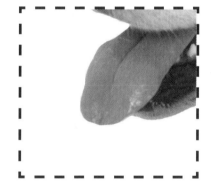

page 28

page 34

Cutouts for Unit 4

page 42

page 46

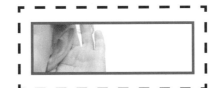

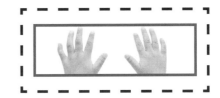

Cutouts for Unit 5

page 52

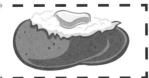

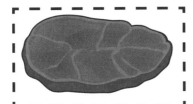

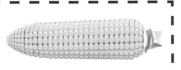

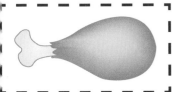

page 54

✂ Cutouts for Unit 6

page 65

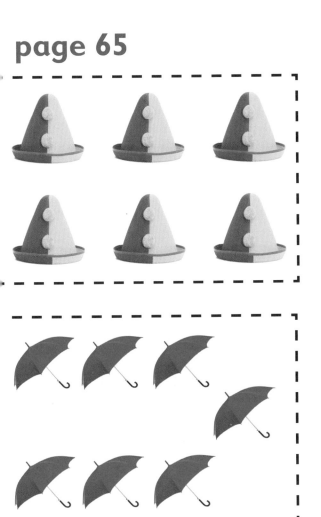

page 66

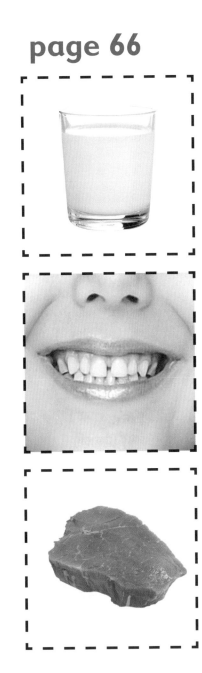

page 70

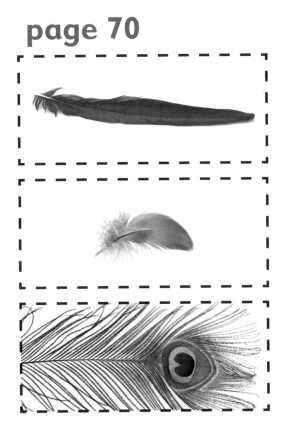

 # Cutouts for Unit 7

page 77

page 78

page 82

 # Cutouts for Unit 8

page 89

page 90

page 94